FISH NUMBER TRACING

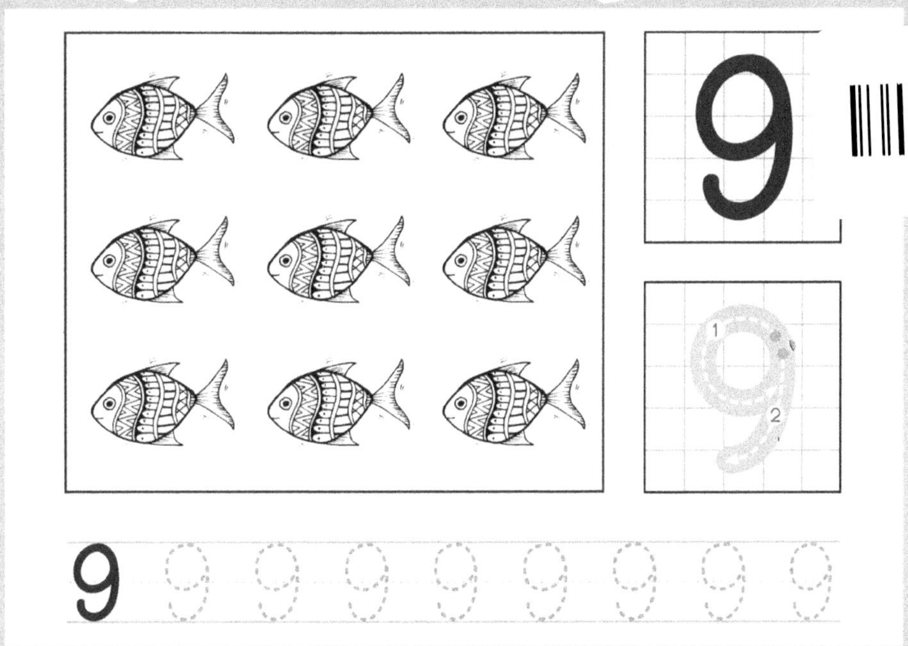

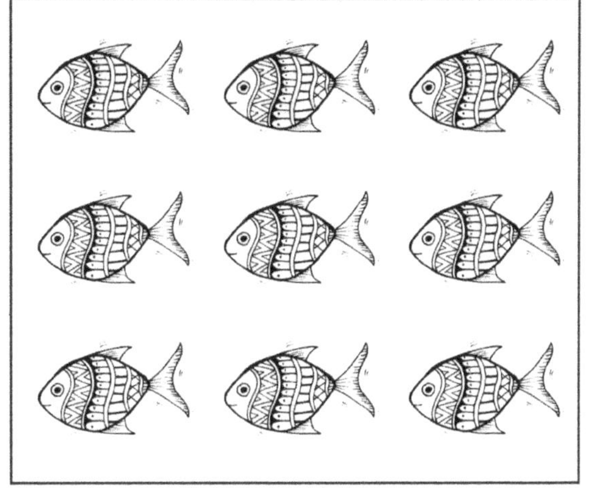

AF441562

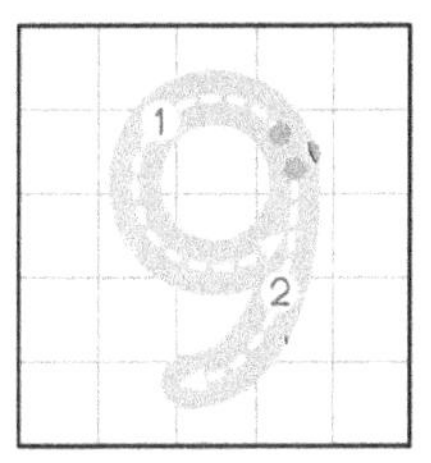

9

FOR PRESCHOOLERS:

LEARN TO WRITE FOR KIDS AGES 3-5 AND KINDERGARTEN

SEAN WOO

EMAIL US AT:

journal@books13.com

TO GET FREE GOODIES!

****

Just title the email "Number Tracing!"
And we will send some extra surprises!

THIS BOOK BELONGS TO:

____

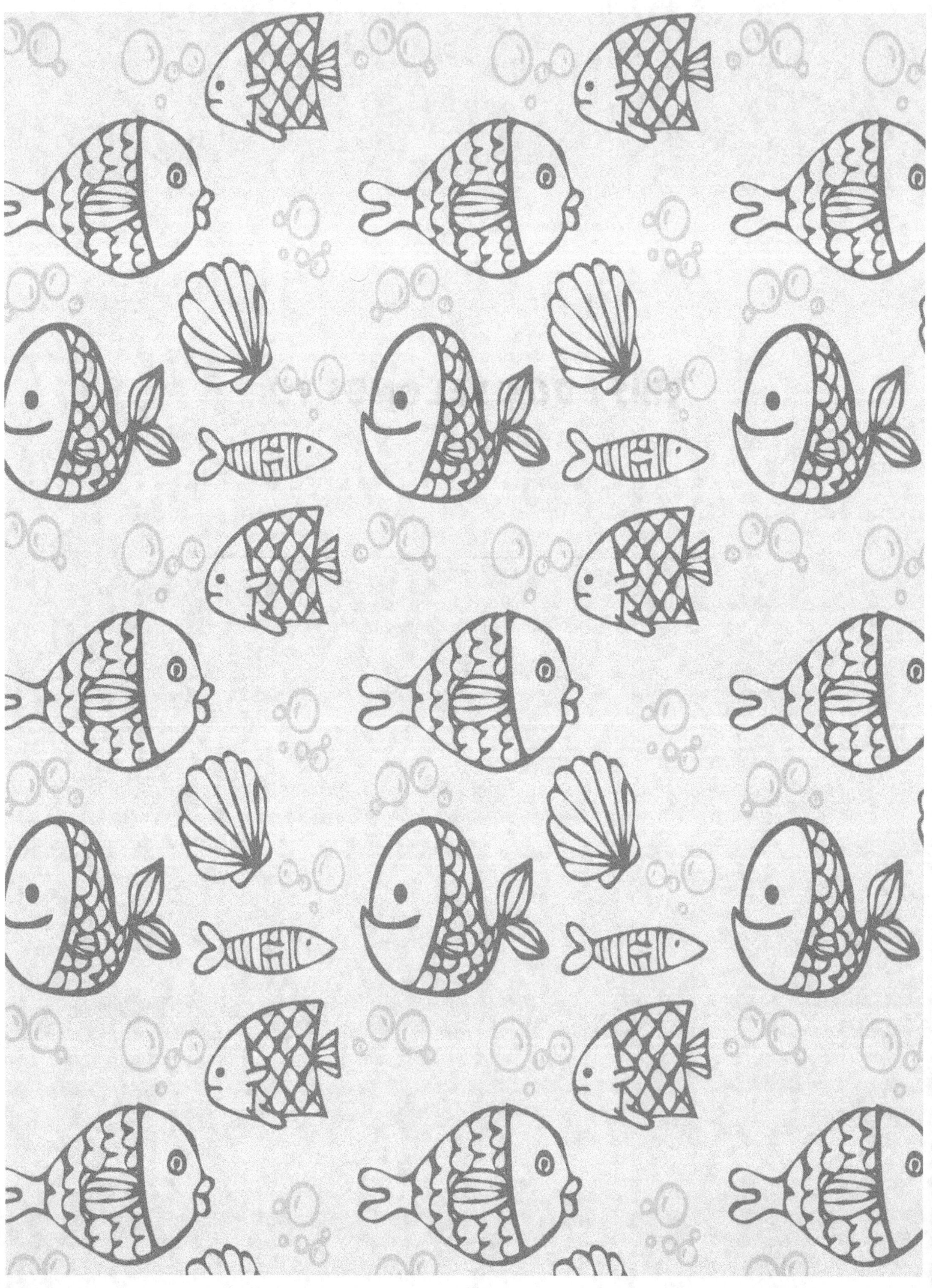

TRACE THE NUMBER

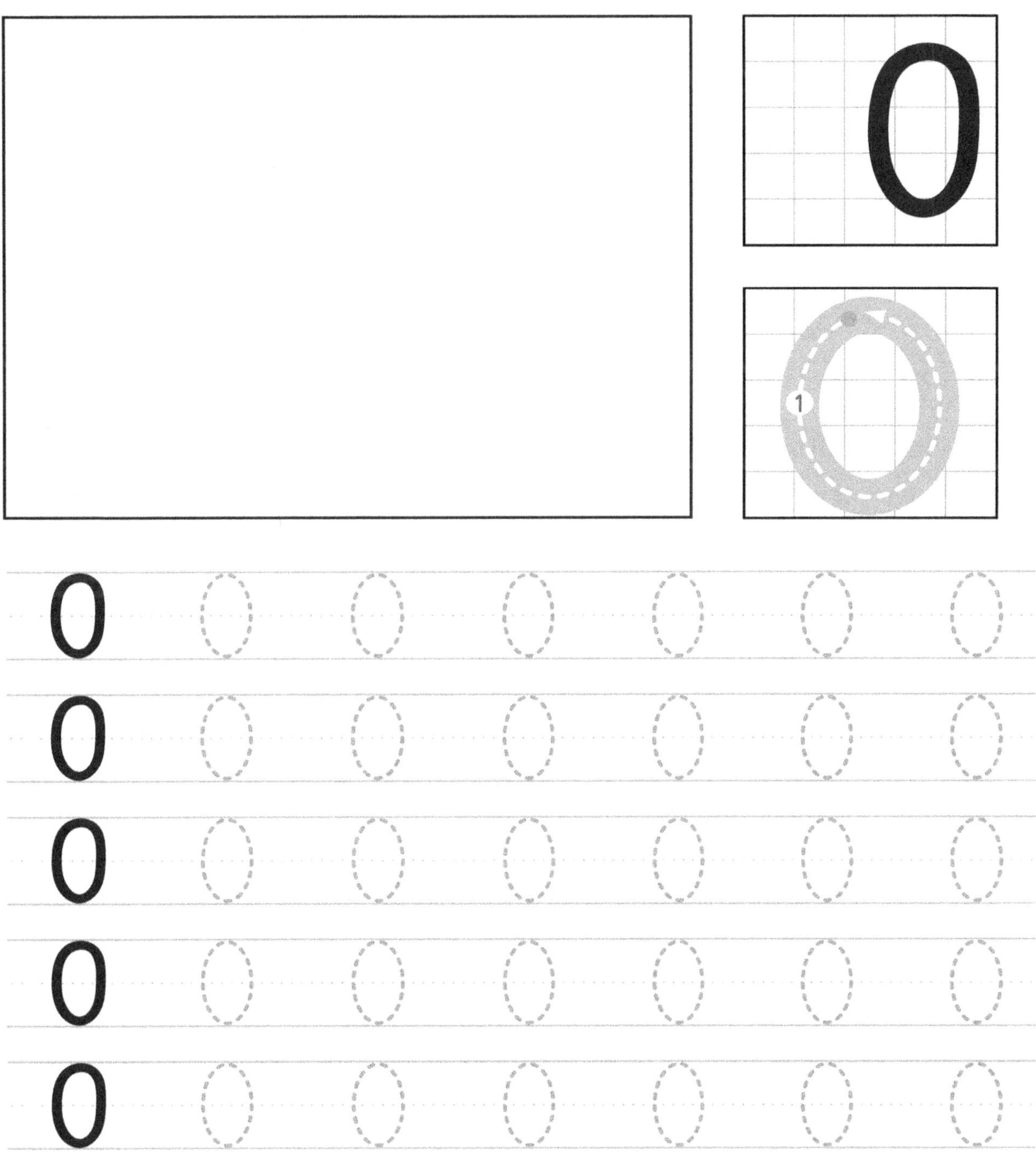

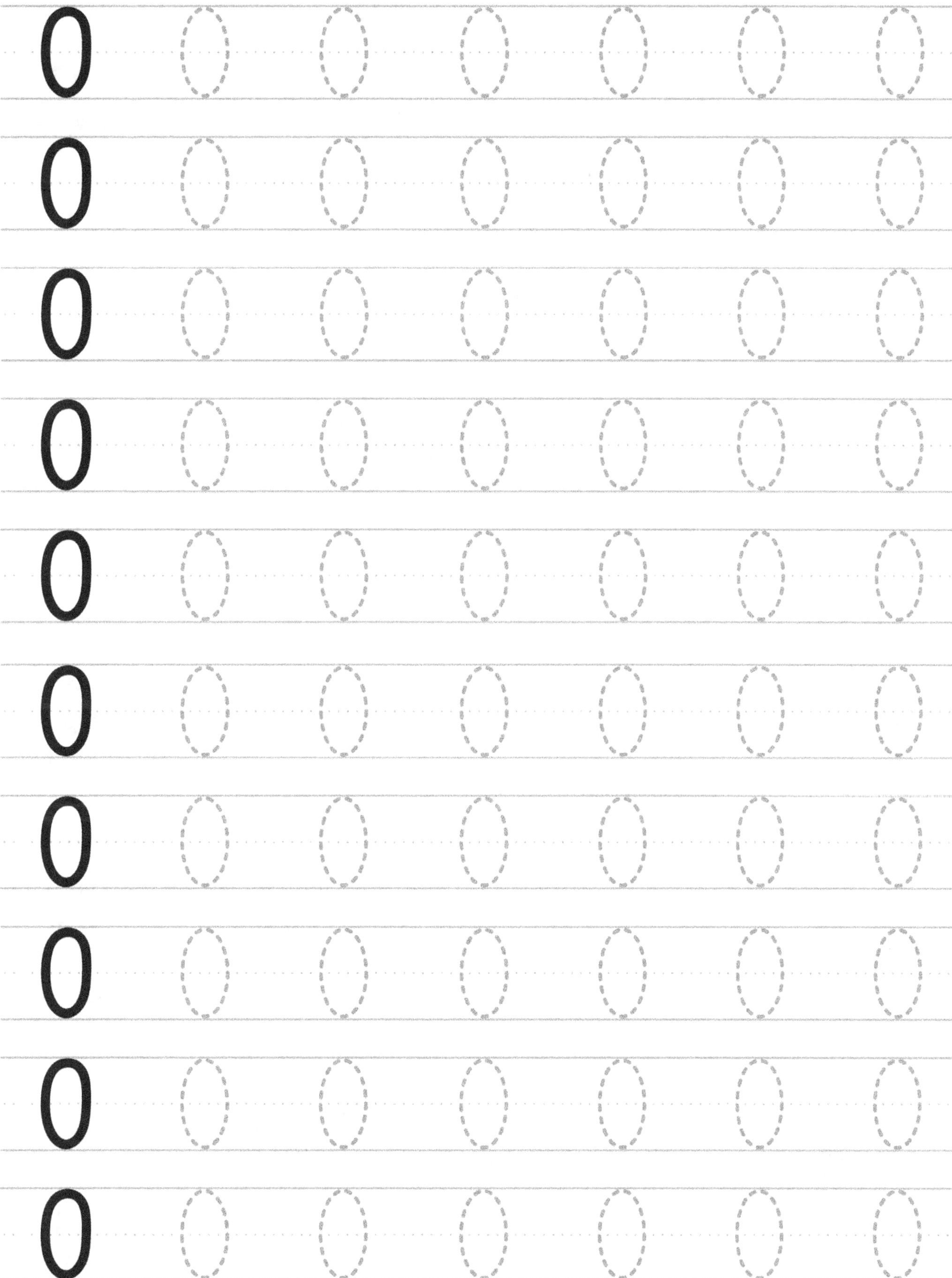

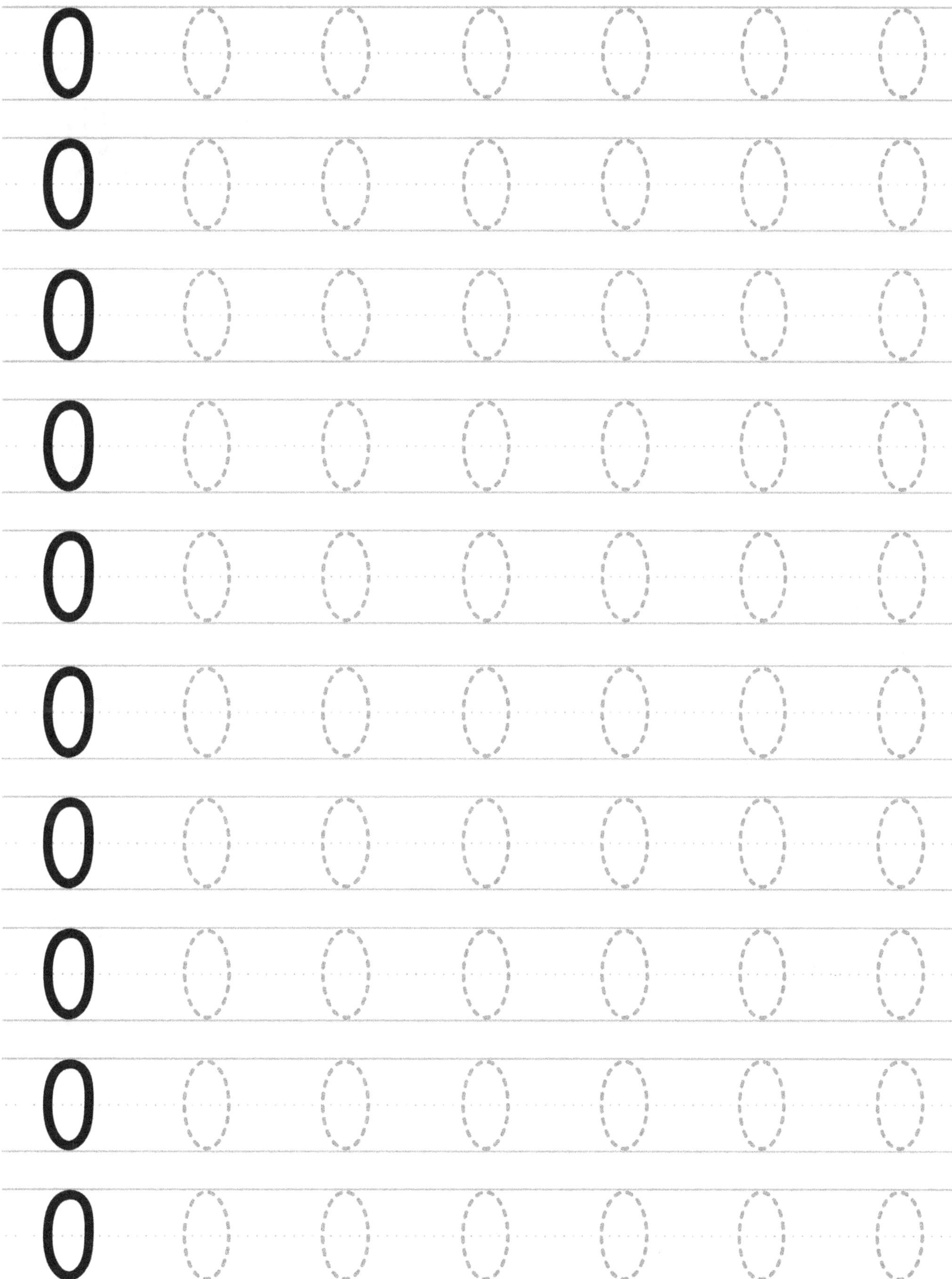

TRACE THE NUMBER

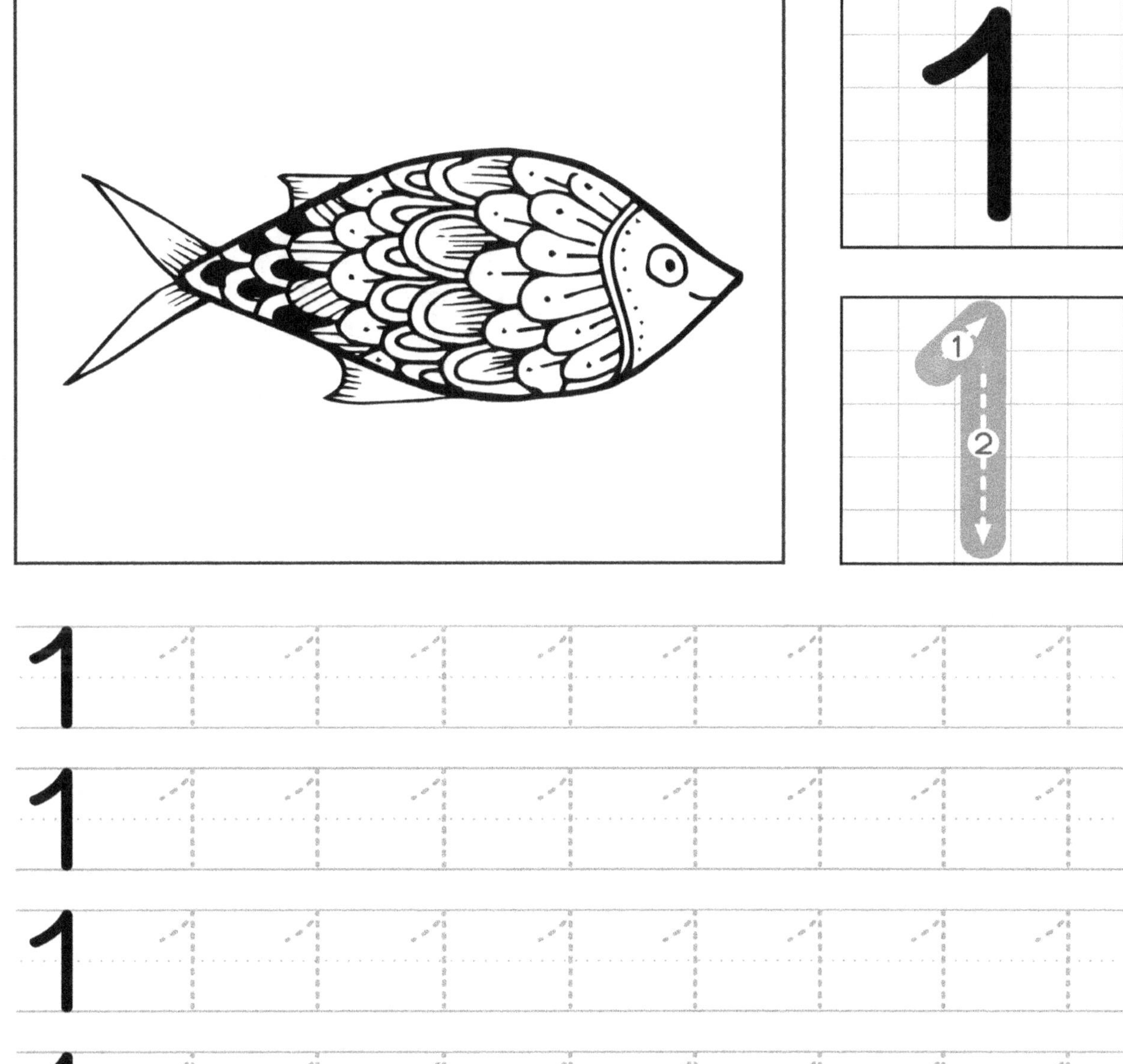

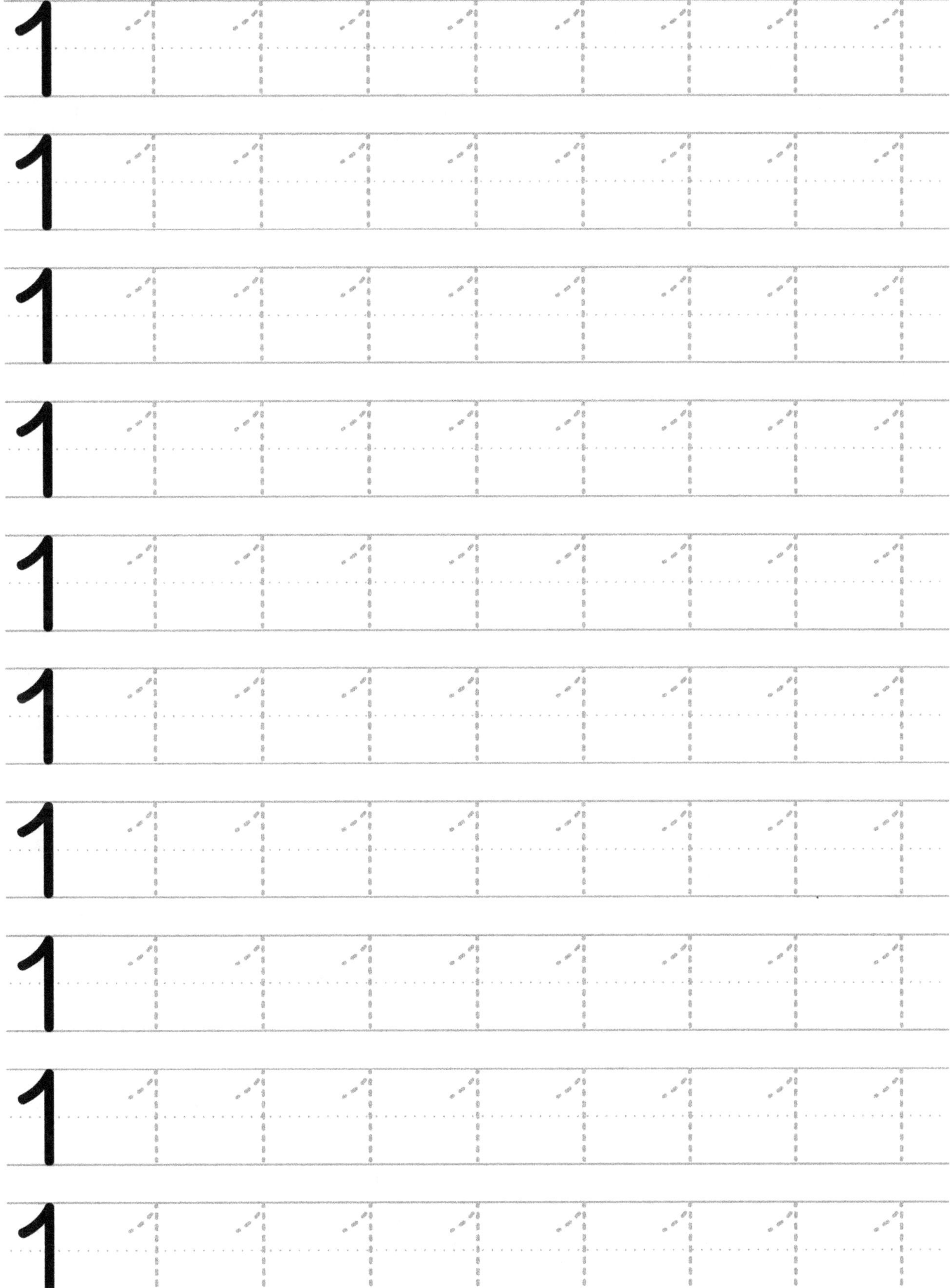

1

1

1

1

1

1

1

1

1

1

TRACE THE NUMBER

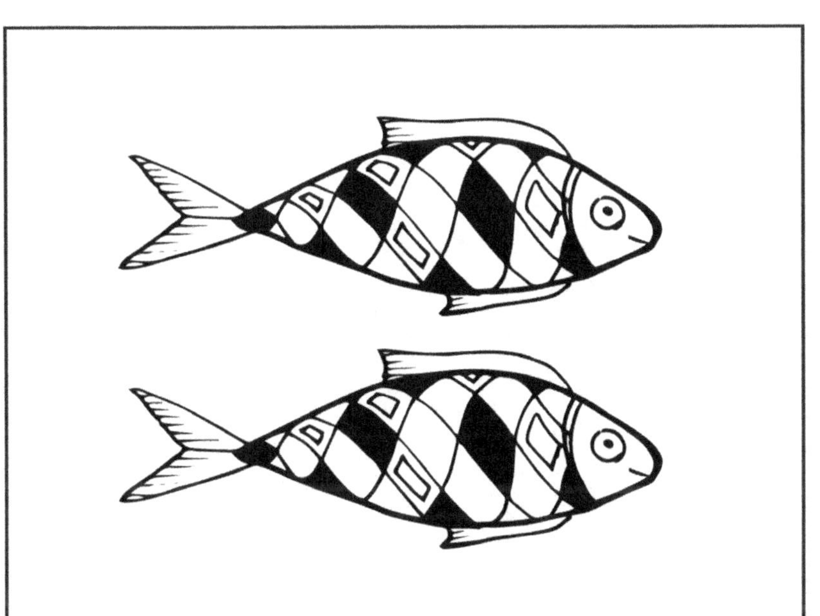

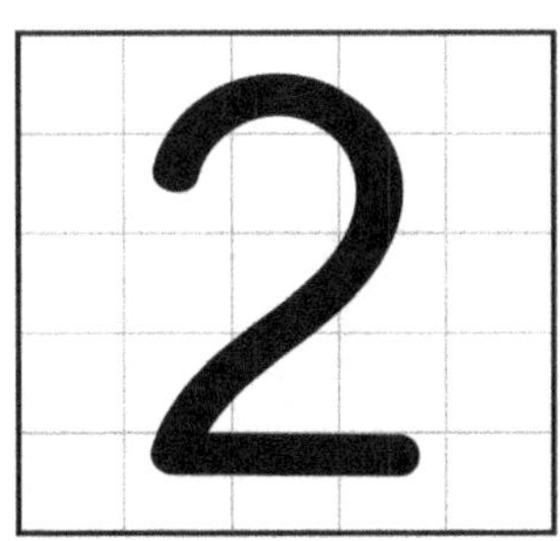

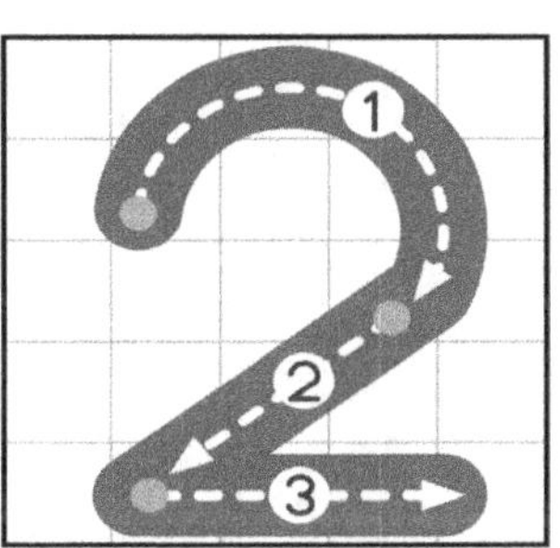

2 2 2 2 2 2 2 2 2

2 2 2 2 2 2 2 2 2

2 2 2 2 2 2 2 2 2

2 2 2 2 2 2 2 2 2

2 2 2 2 2 2 2 2 2

2 2 2 2 2 2 2 2 2

2 2 2 2 2 2 2 2 2

2 2 2 2 2 2 2 2 2

2 2 2 2 2 2 2 2 2

2 2 2 2 2 2 2 2 2

2 2 2 2 2 2 2 2 2

2 2 2 2 2 2 2 2 2

2 2 2 2 2 2 2 2 2

2 2 2 2 2 2 2 2 2

2 2 2 2 2 2 2 2 2

2 2 2 2 2 2 2 2 2

2 2 2 2 2 2 2 2 2

2 2 2 2 2 2 2 2 2

2 2 2 2 2 2 2 2 2

2 2 2 2 2 2 2 2 2

2 2 2 2 2 2 2 2 2

2 2 2 2 2 2 2 2 2

2 2 2 2 2 2 2 2 2

2 2 2 2 2 2 2 2 2

2 2 2 2 2 2 2 2 2

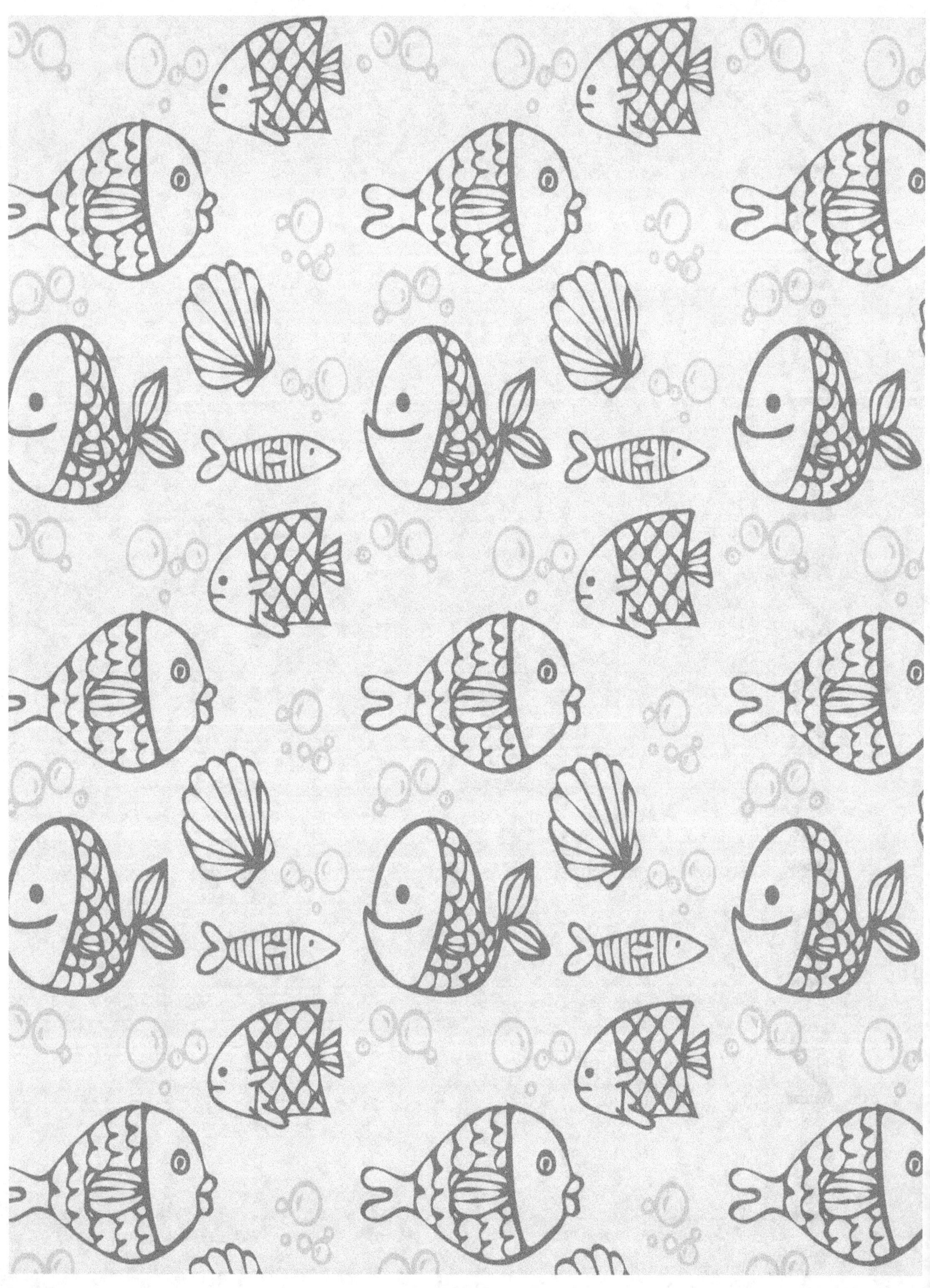

TRACE THE NUMBER

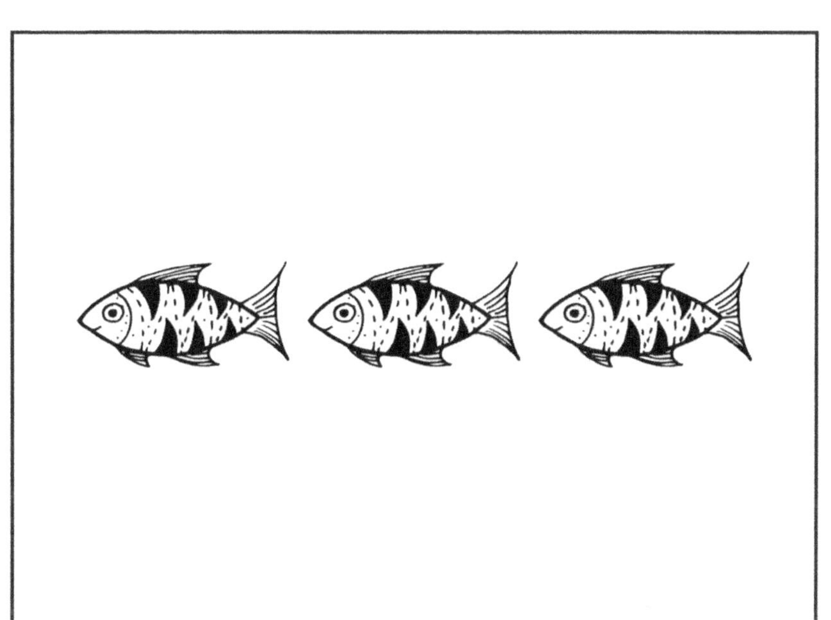

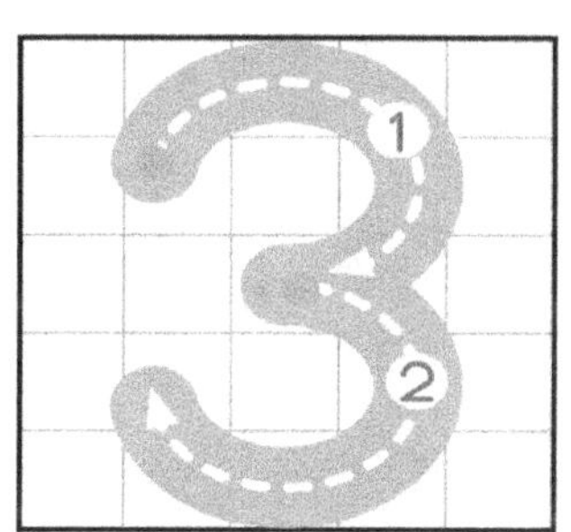

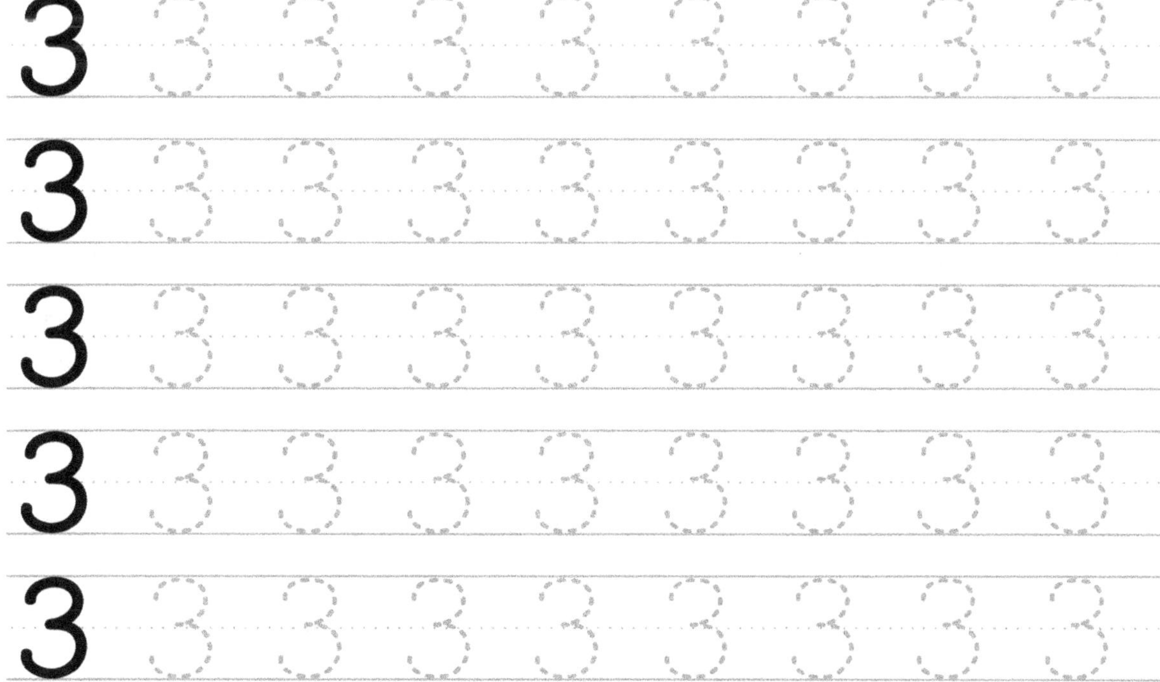

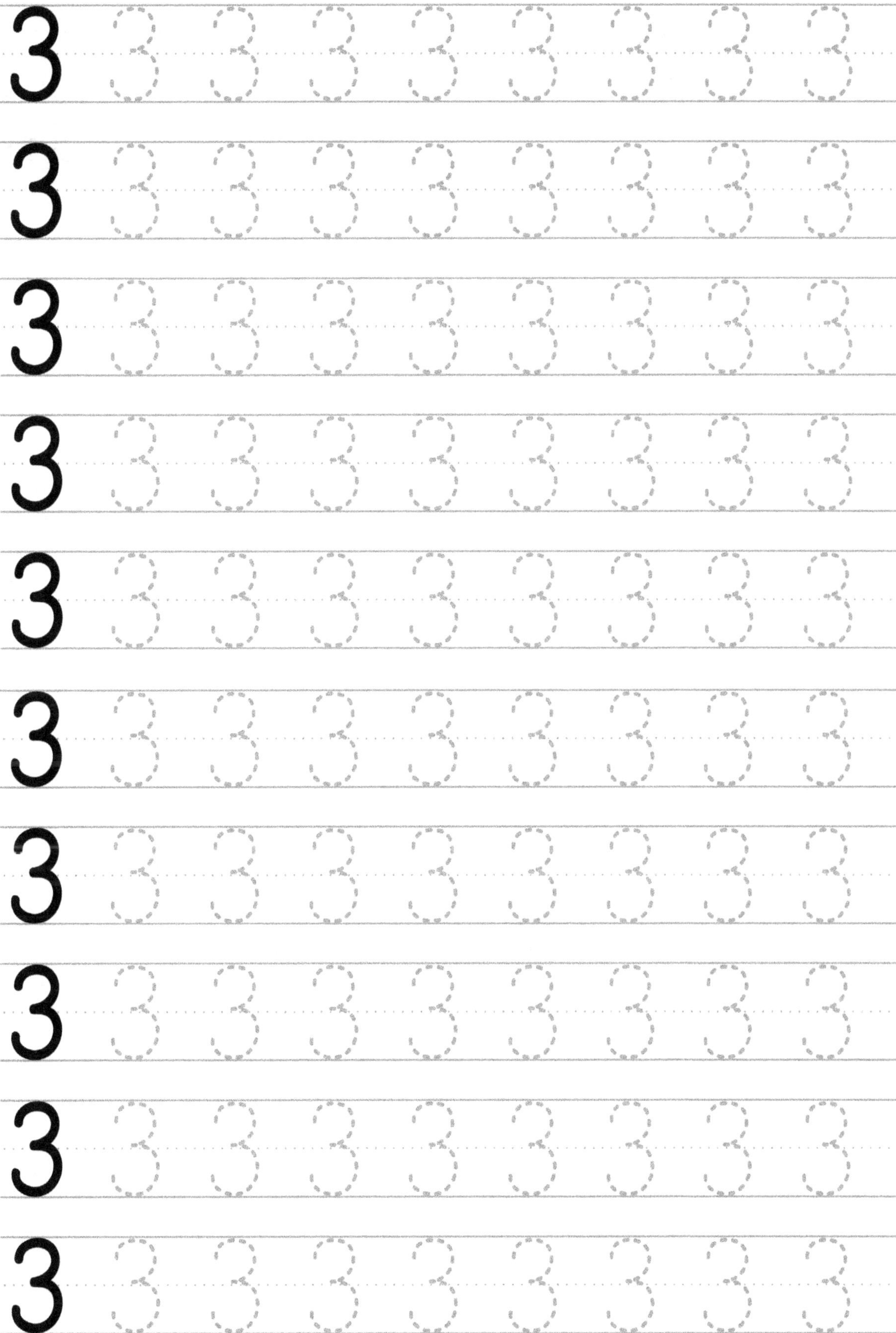

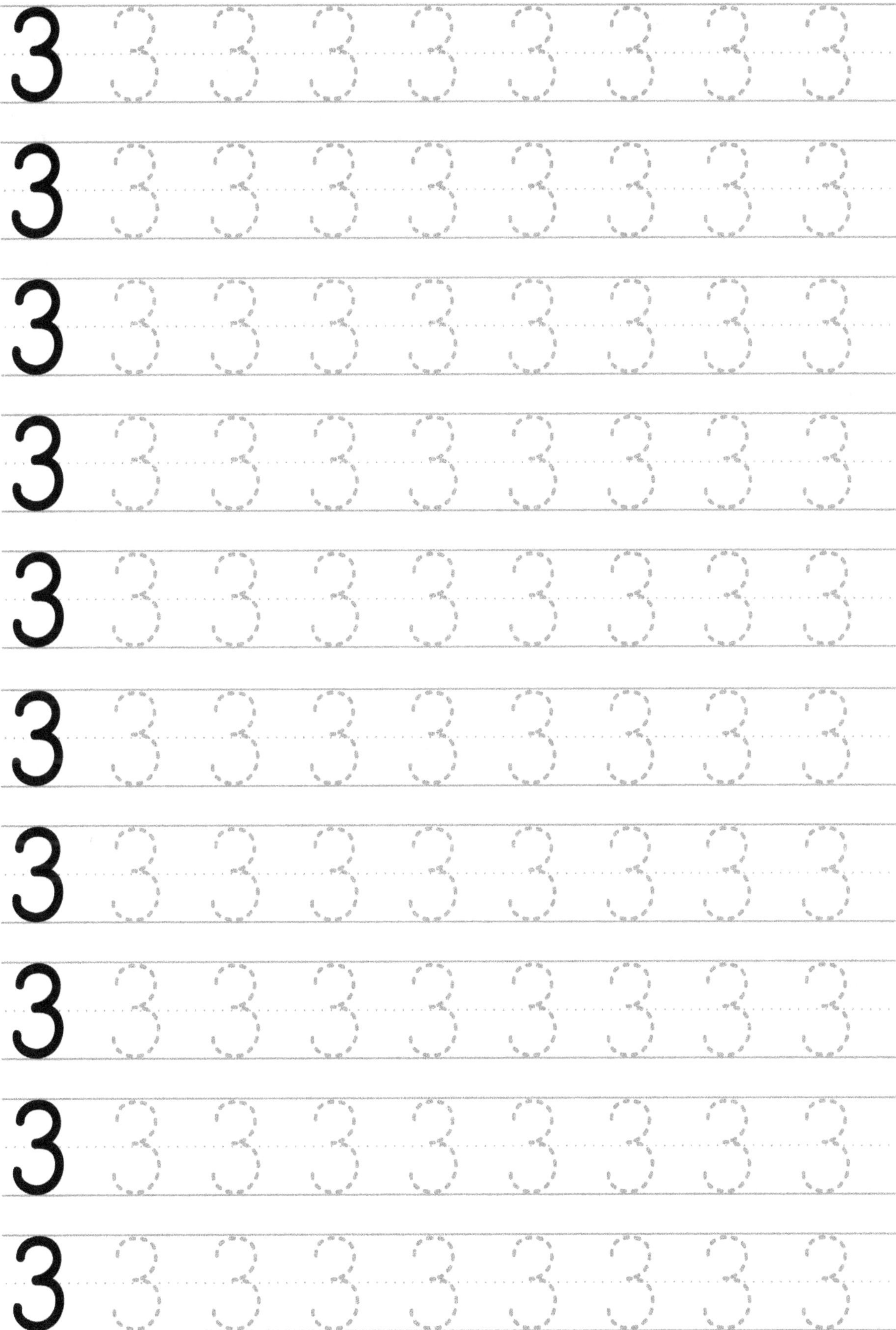

TRACE THE NUMBER

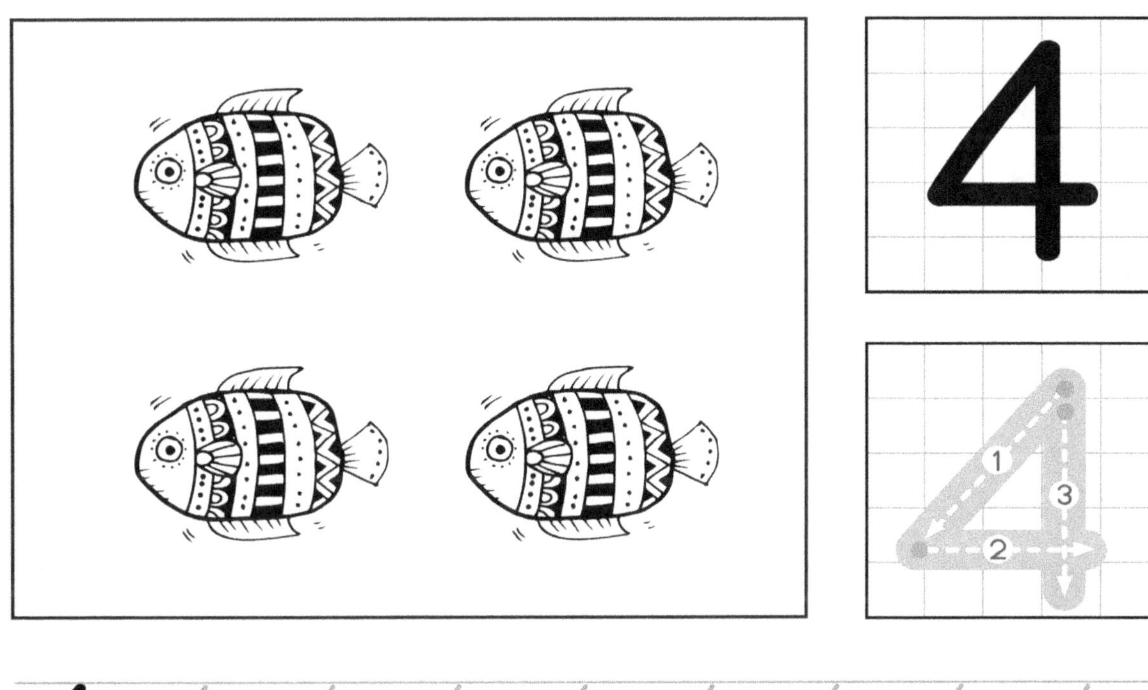

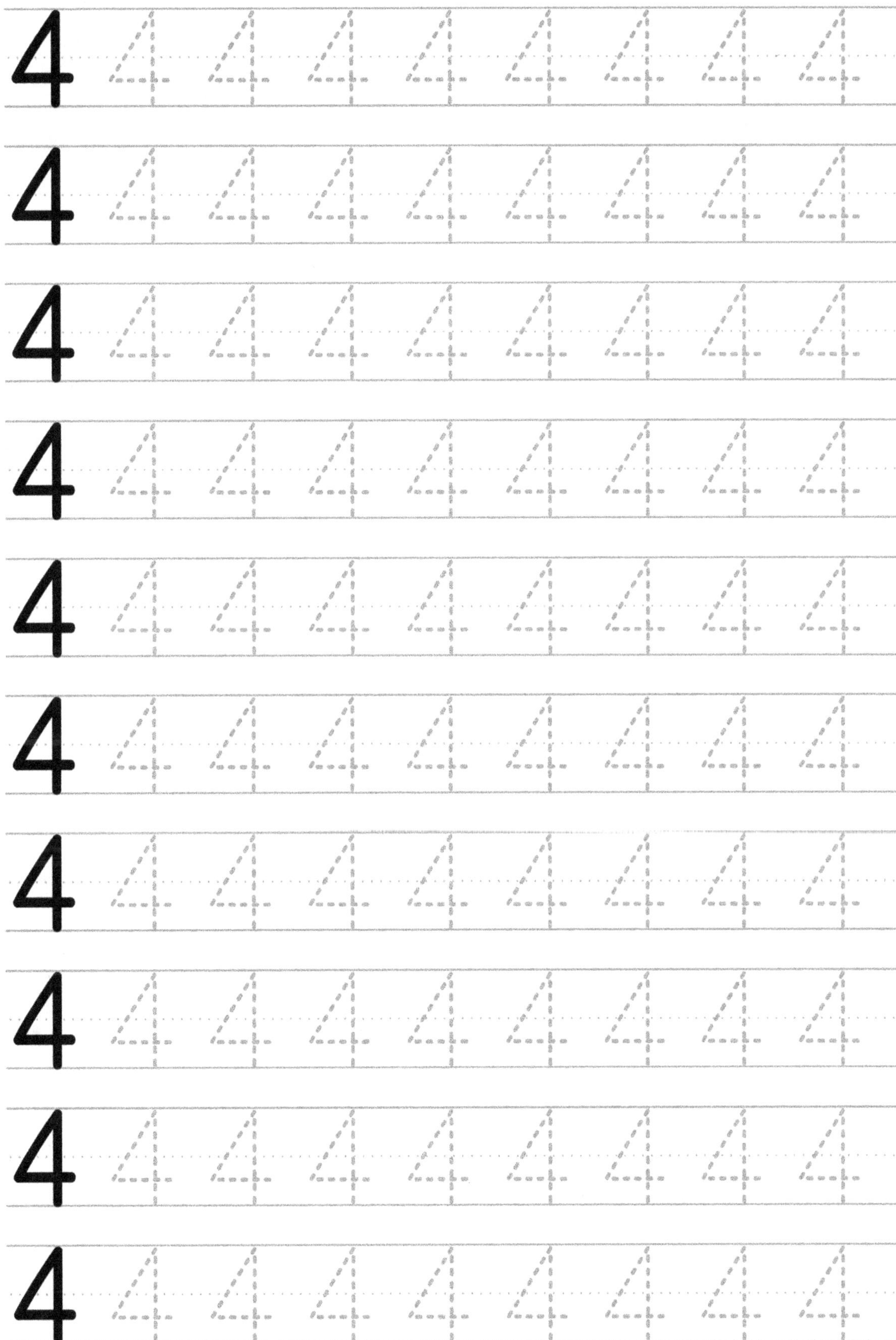

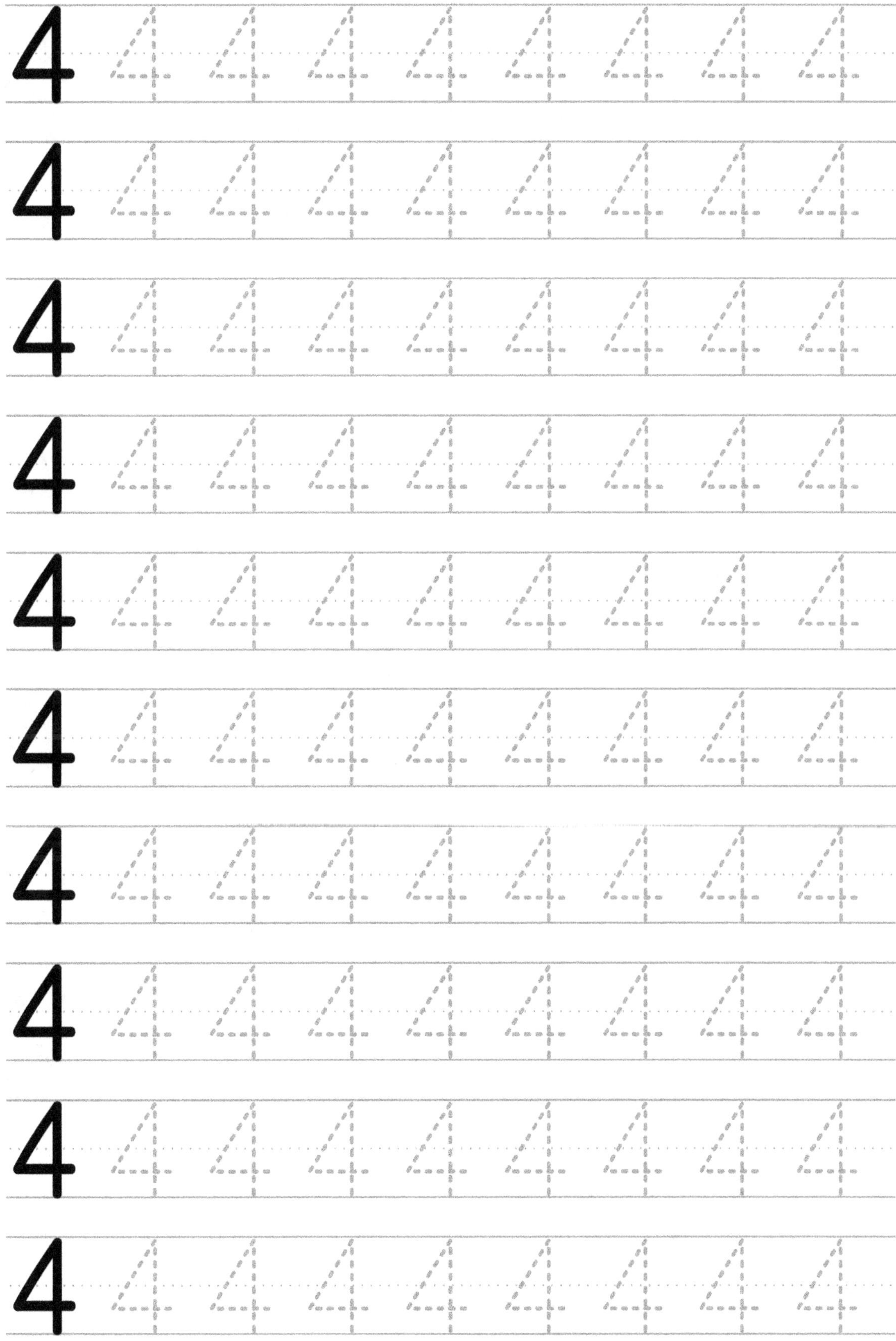

TRACE THE NUMBER

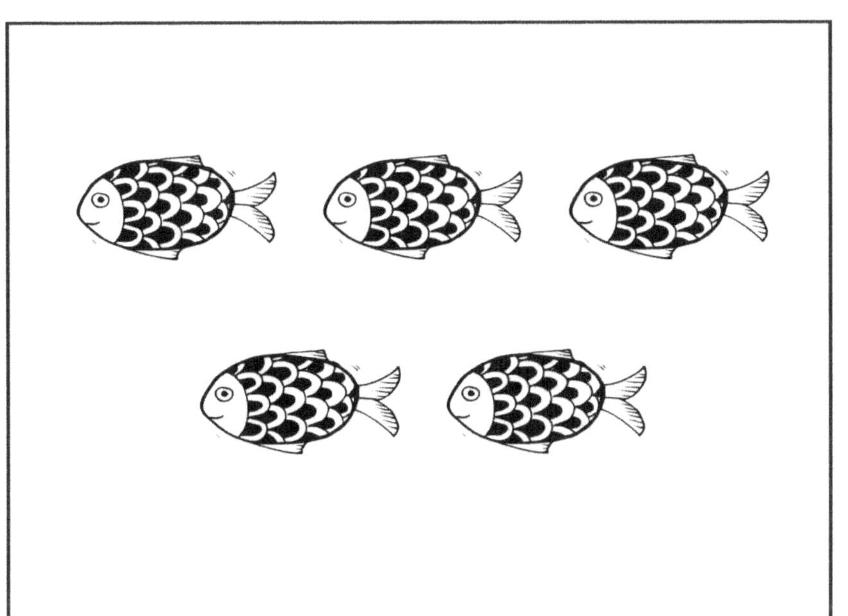

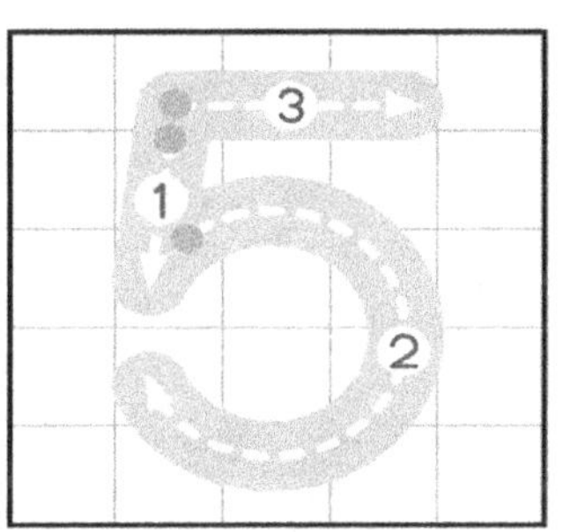

5

5

5

5

5

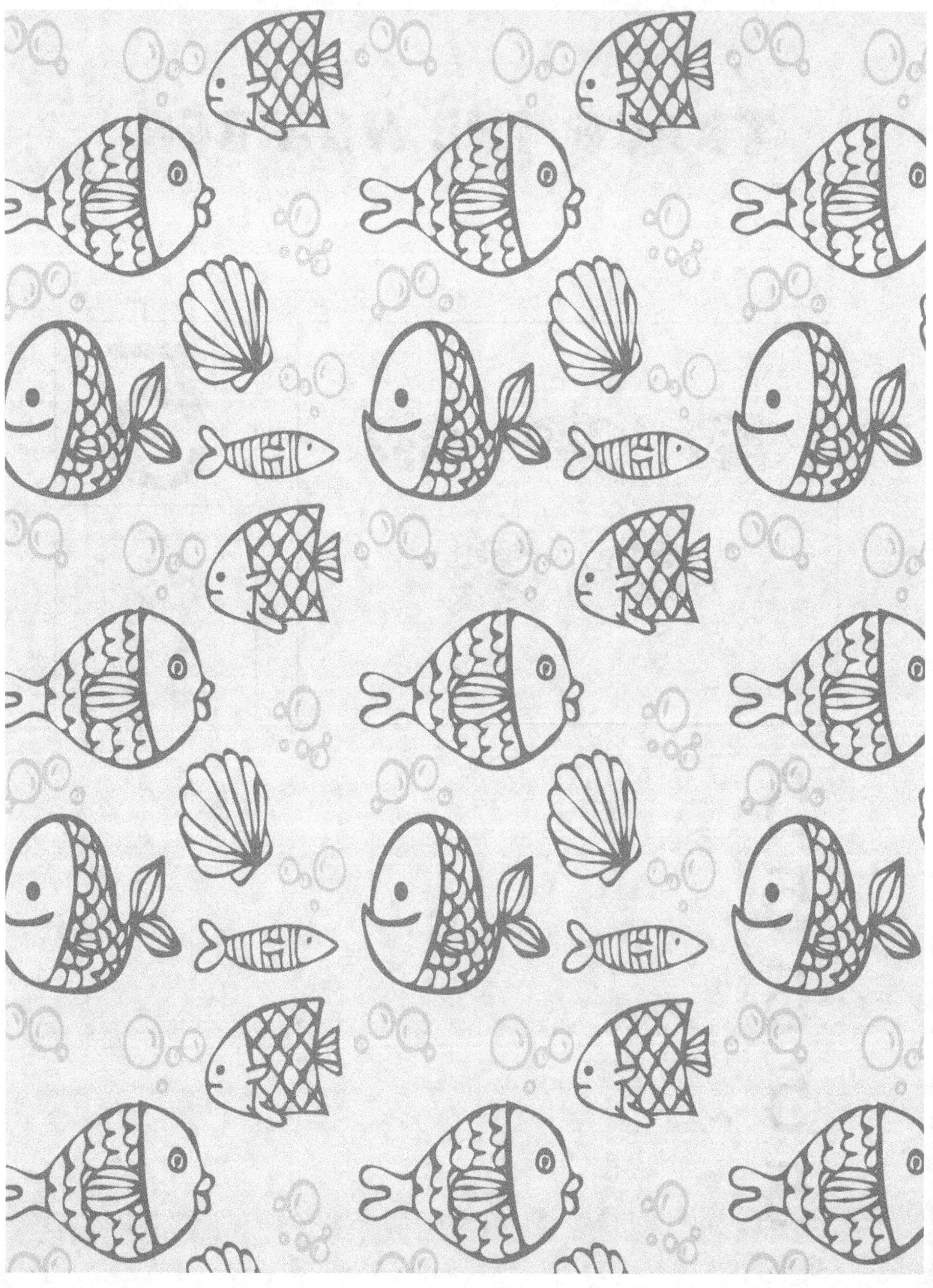

5 5 5 5 5 5 5 5

5 5 5 5 5 5 5 5

5 5 5 5 5 5 5 5

5 5 5 5 5 5 5 5

5 5 5 5 5 5 5 5

5 5 5 5 5 5 5 5

5 5 5 5 5 5 5 5

5 5 5 5 5 5 5 5

5 5 5 5 5 5 5 5

5 5 5 5 5 5 5 5

5 5 5 5 5 5 5 5

5 5 5 5 5 5 5 5

5 5 5 5 5 5 5 5

5 5 5 5 5 5 5 5

5 5 5 5 5 5 5 5

5 5 5 5 5 5 5 5

5 5 5 5 5 5 5 5

5 5 5 5 5 5 5 5

5 5 5 5 5 5 5 5

5 5 5 5 5 5 5 5

TRACE THE NUMBER

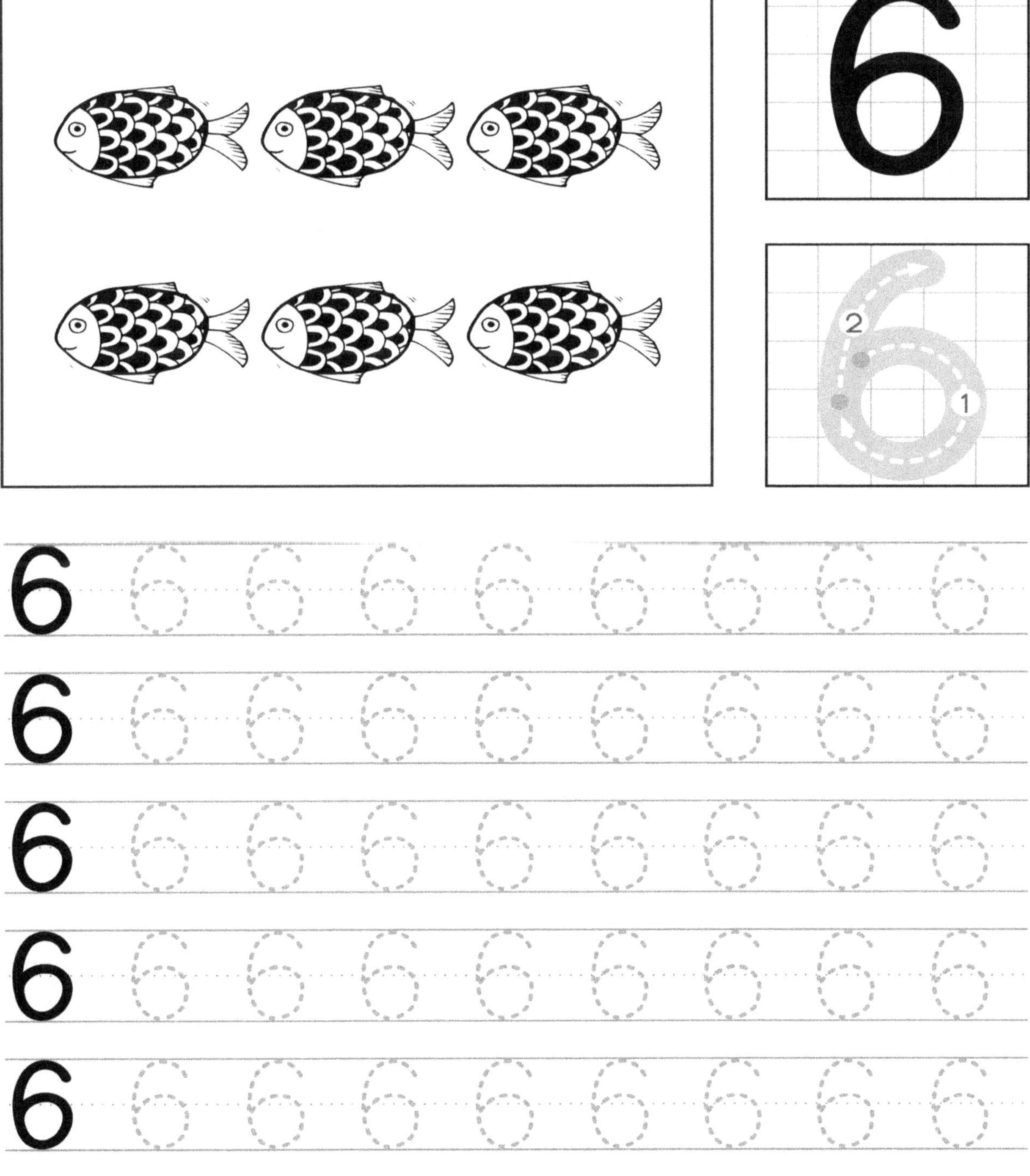

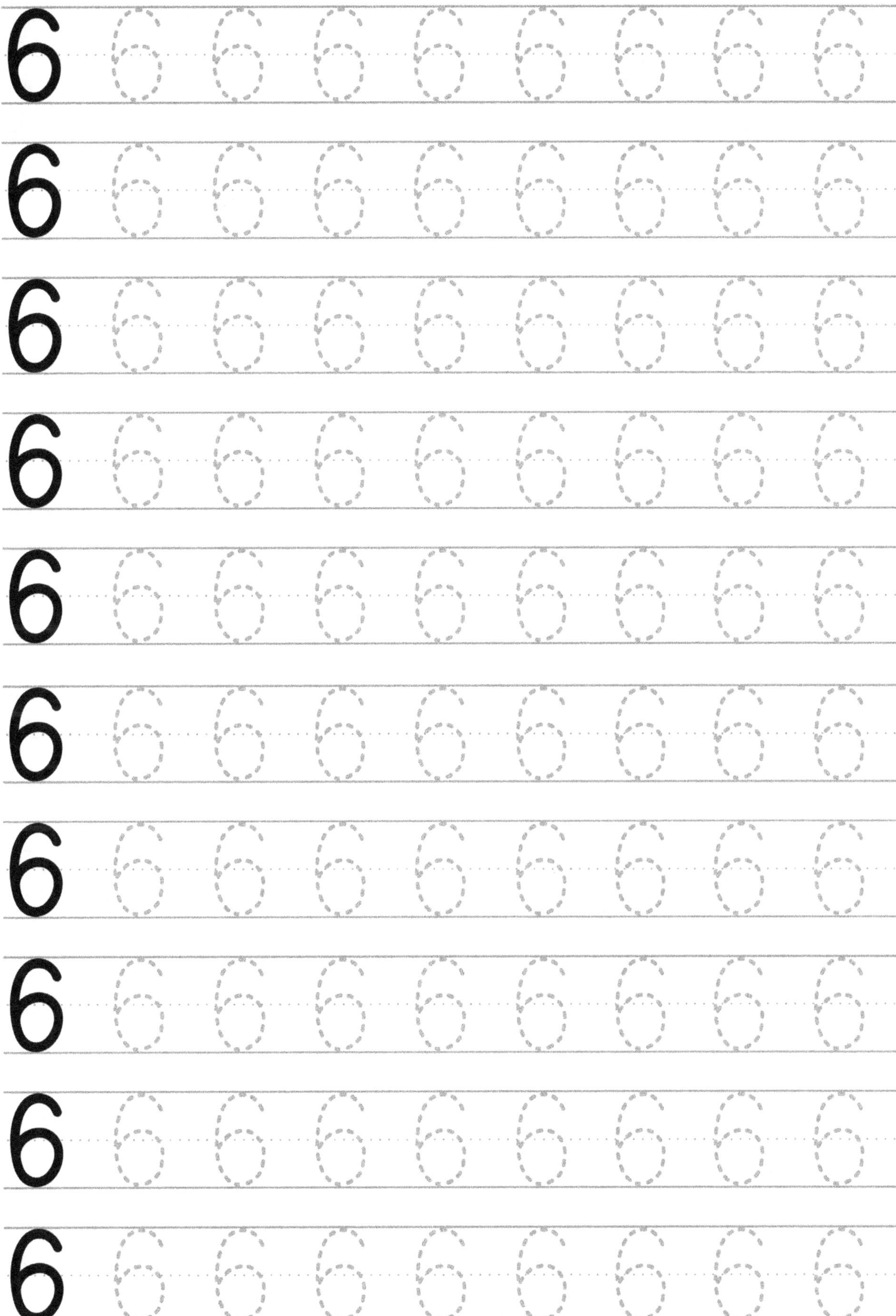

6 6 6 6 6 6 6 6 6

6 6 6 6 6 6 6 6 6

6 6 6 6 6 6 6 6 6

6 6 6 6 6 6 6 6 6

6 6 6 6 6 6 6 6 6

6 6 6 6 6 6 6 6 6

6 6 6 6 6 6 6 6 6

6 6 6 6 6 6 6 6 6

6 6 6 6 6 6 6 6 6

6 6 6 6 6 6 6 6 6

TRACE THE NUMBER

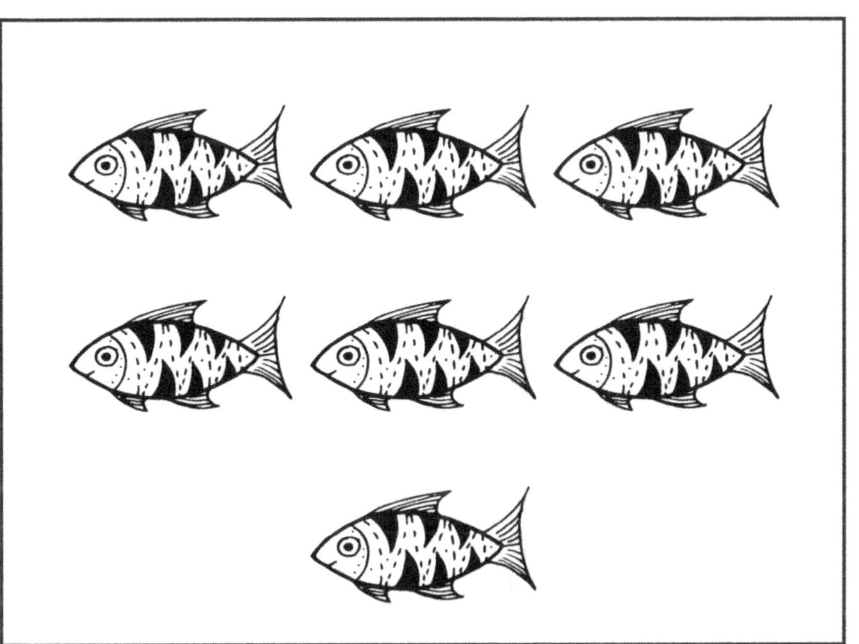

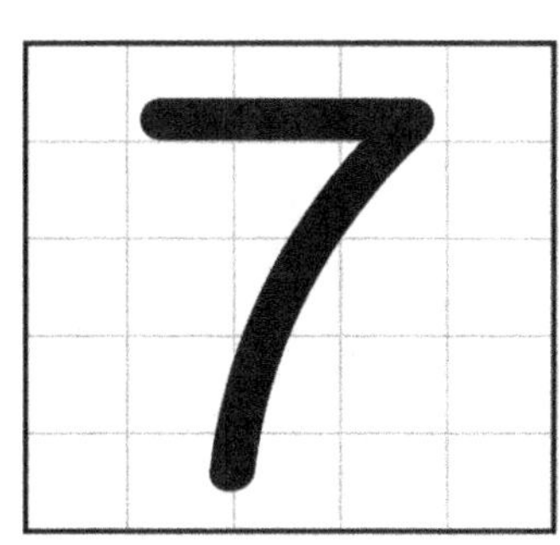

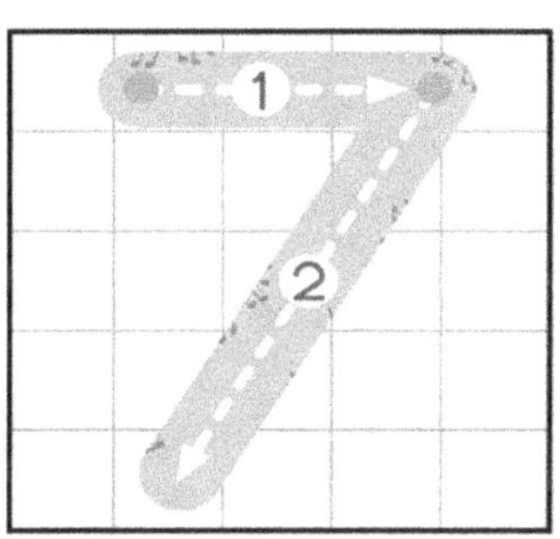

7

7

7

7

7

7

7

7

7

7

7

7

7

7

7

7

7

7

7

7

7

7

7

7

7

TRACE THE NUMBER

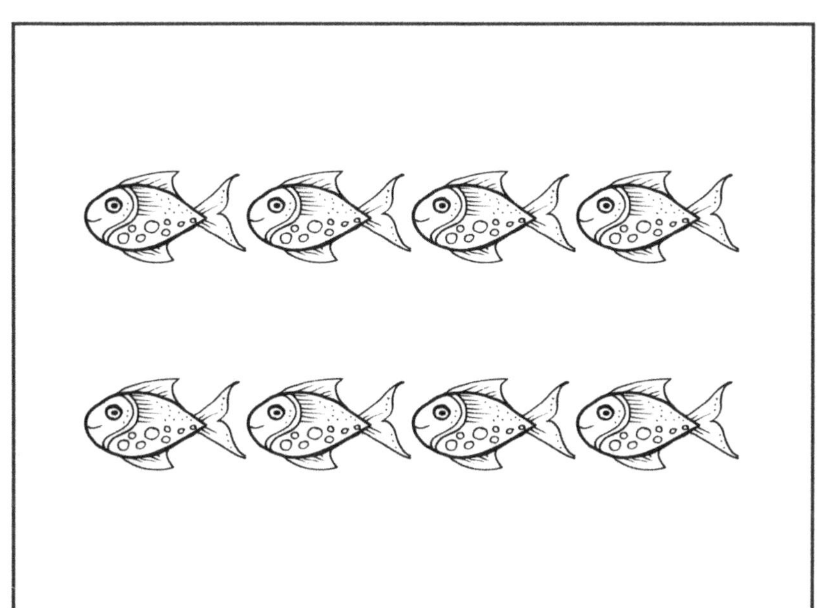

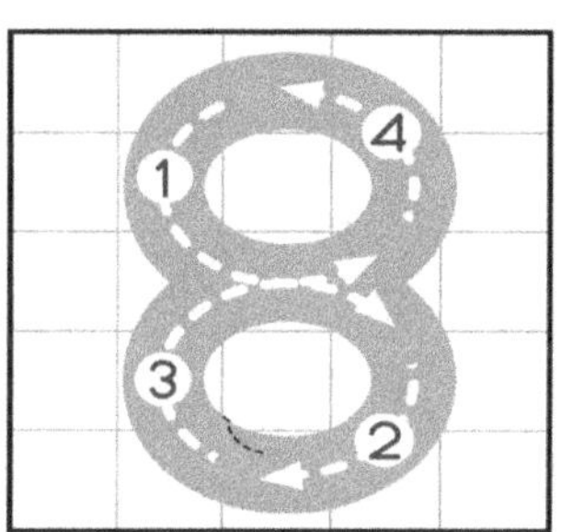

TRACE THE NUMBER

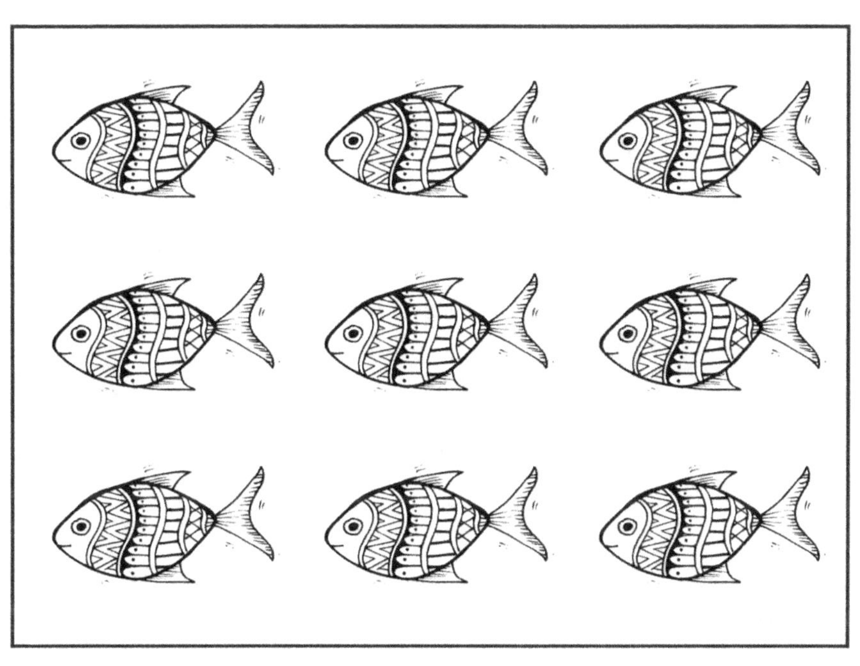

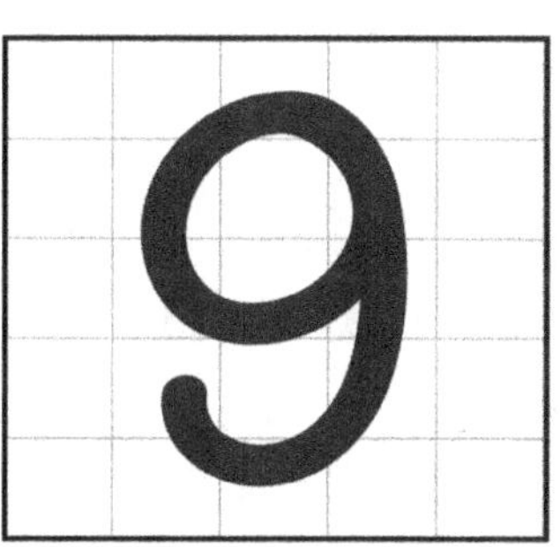

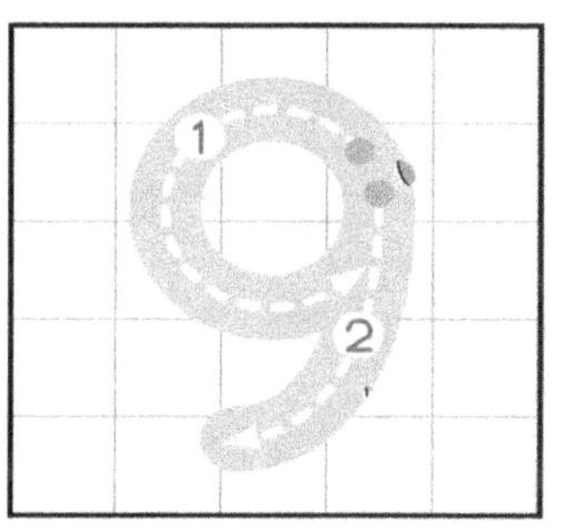

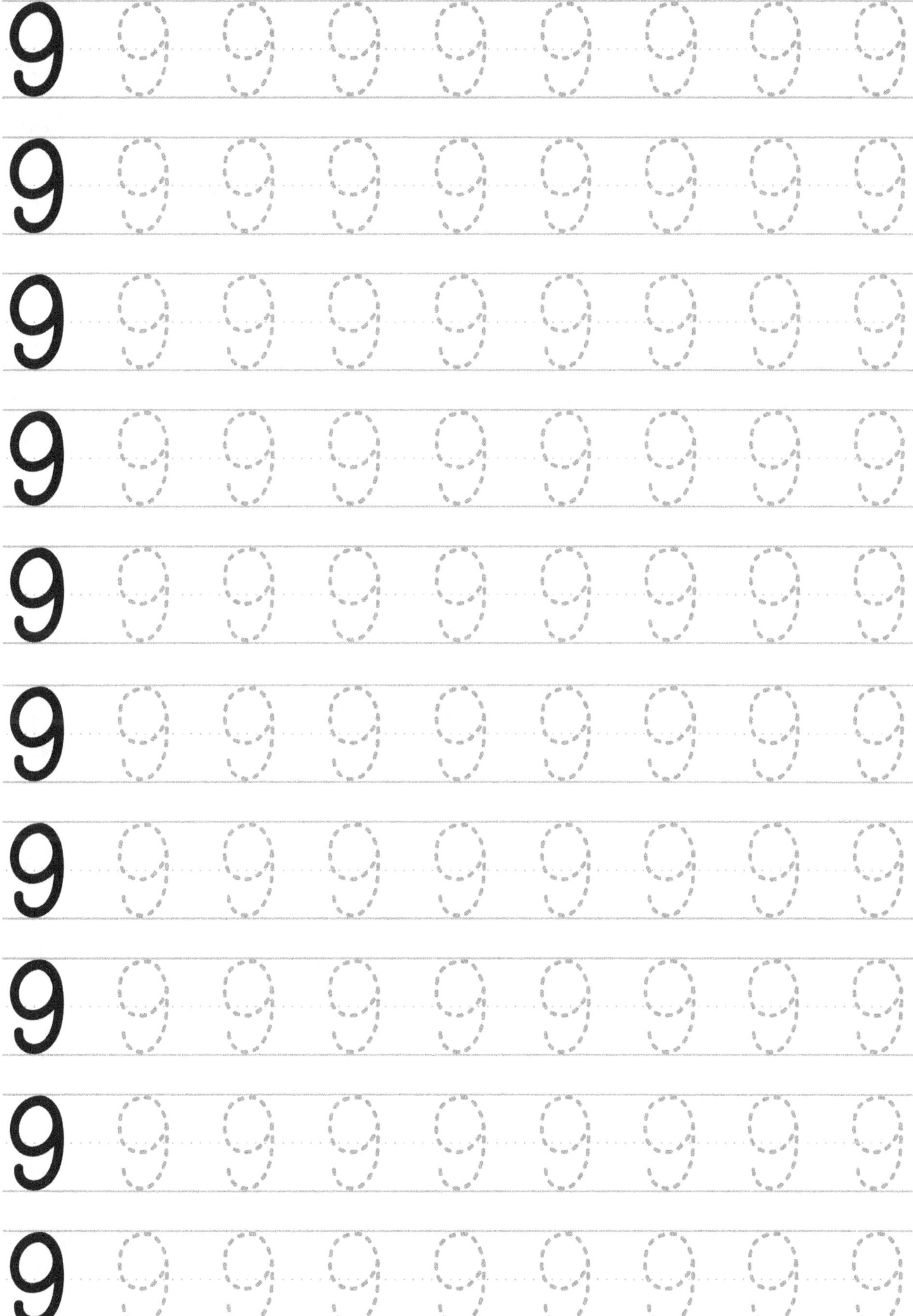

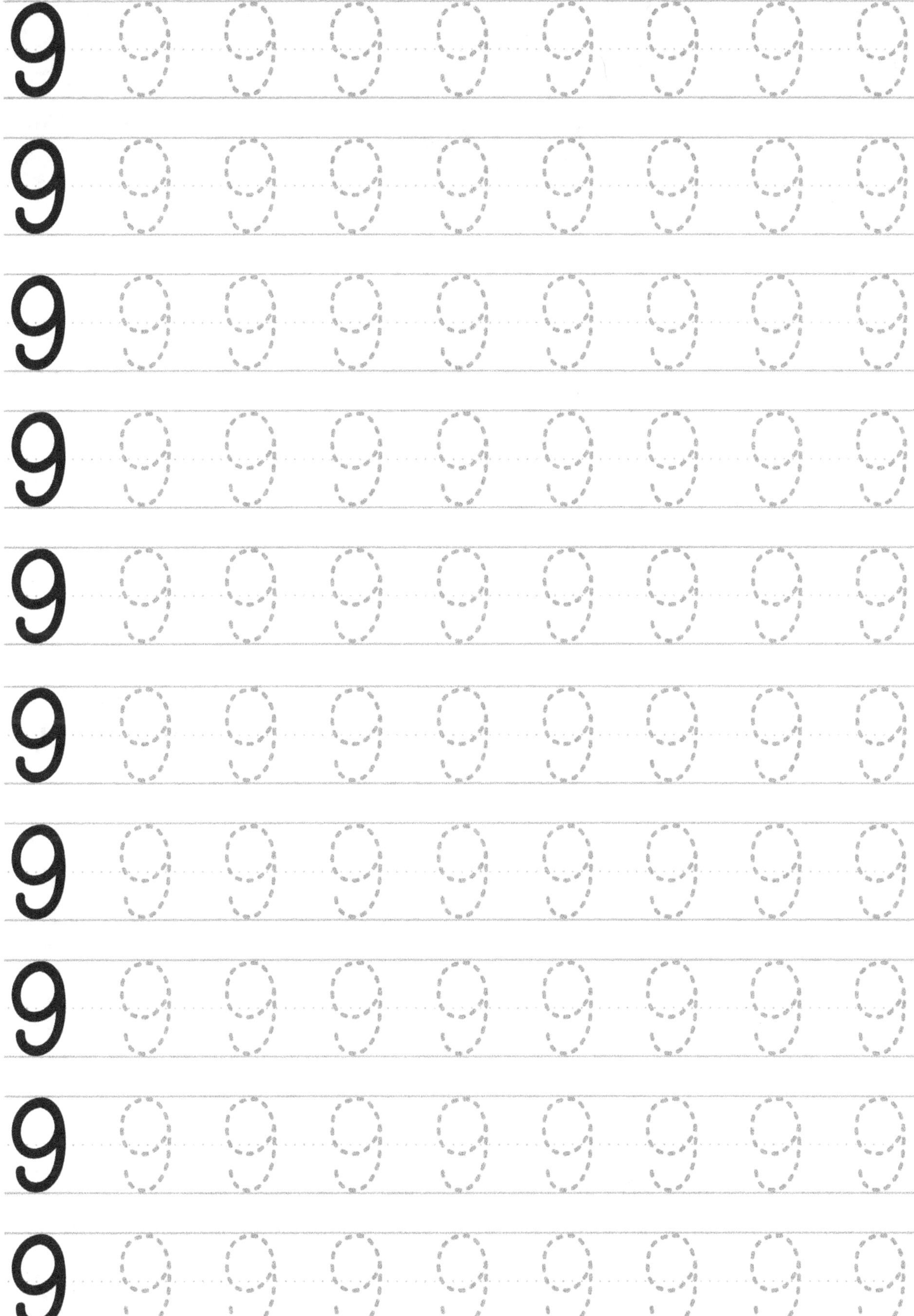

TRACE THE NUMBER

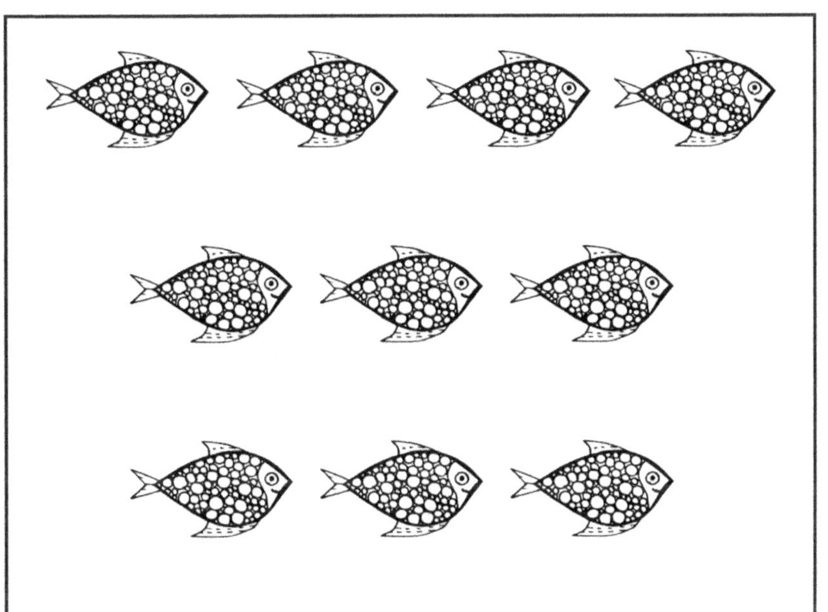

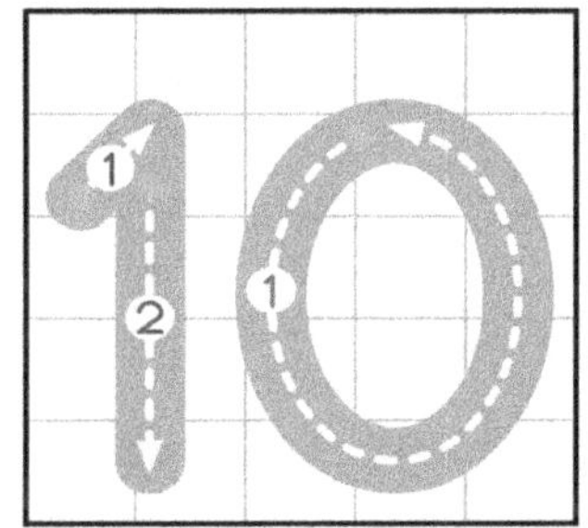

10

10

10

10

10

10 10 10 10 10 10 10

10 10 10 10 10 10 10

10 10 10 10 10 10 10

10 10 10 10 10 10 10

10 10 10 10 10 10 10

10 10 10 10 10 10 10

10 10 10 10 10 10 10

10 10 10 10 10 10 10

10 10 10 10 10 10 10

10 10 10 10 10 10 10

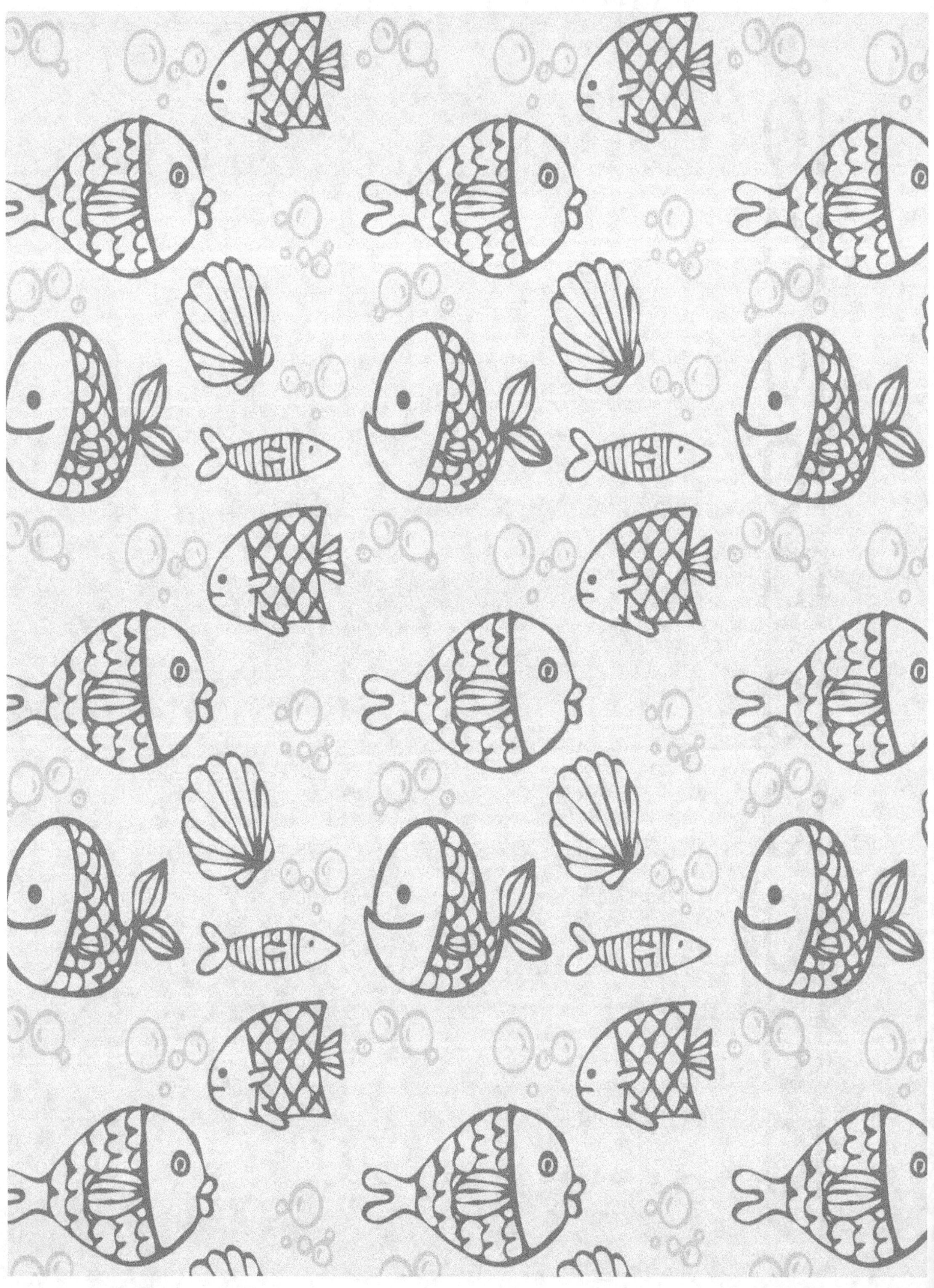

www.ingramcontent.com/pod-product-compliance
Lightning Source LLC
Chambersburg PA
CBHW080741180726
48003CB00023B/3276

* 9 7 9 8 6 4 2 2 5 5 6 9 8 *